SEA LIONS

LIVING WILD

Published by Creative Education
P.O. Box 227, Mankato, Minnesota 56002
Creative Education is an imprint of The Creative Company
www.thecreativecompany.us

Design and production by Mary Herrmann
Art direction by Rita Marshall
Printed in the United States of America

Photographs by Alamy (Accent Alaska.com, Alaska Stock, Brandon Cole Marine
Photography, imagebroker, Photos 12, Jeff Rotman, Robert Stainforth, Travelpix), Corbis
(Paul Thompson), Dreamstime (Steve Allen, Bernard Breton, Michael Elliott, Gvision,
Derek Holzapfel, Irina Igumnova, Jmjm, Burt Johnson, Robert Johnson, Lindamore,
Christian Schmalhofer, Smellme, Laurel Stewart, Bob Suir, Mogens Trolle, Ivonne
Wierink), Getty Images (Sylvain Cordier, Sergey Gorshkov, Jens Kuhfs, Silvina Parma),
Shutterstock (Kayla A, Galyna Andrushko, Henk Bentlage, fantuz, Hugh Lansdown,
NatalieJean, naturediver, nouseforname, Katrina Outland, rebvt, Rigucci, stock_shot,
Frank Wasserfuehrer), Wikipedia (Kevin Guertin, U.S. Navy)

Library of Congress Cataloging-in-Publication Data
Gish, Melissa.
Sea lions / by Melissa Gish.
p. cm. — (Living wild)
Includes bibliographical references and index.
Summary: A look at sea lions, including their habitats, physical characteristics such as their
webbed flippers, behaviors, relationships with humans, and threatened status in the world
today.
ISBN 978-1-60818-169-8
1. Sea lions—Juvenile literature. I. Title.

QL737.P63G57 2012
599.79'75—dc23   2011035793

First Edition
9 8 7 6 5 4 3 2 1

 CREATIVE EDUCATION

SEA LIONS

Melissa Gish

On a January day in Lima, Peru, the early morning fog melts away under the sun, revealing the jagged shores

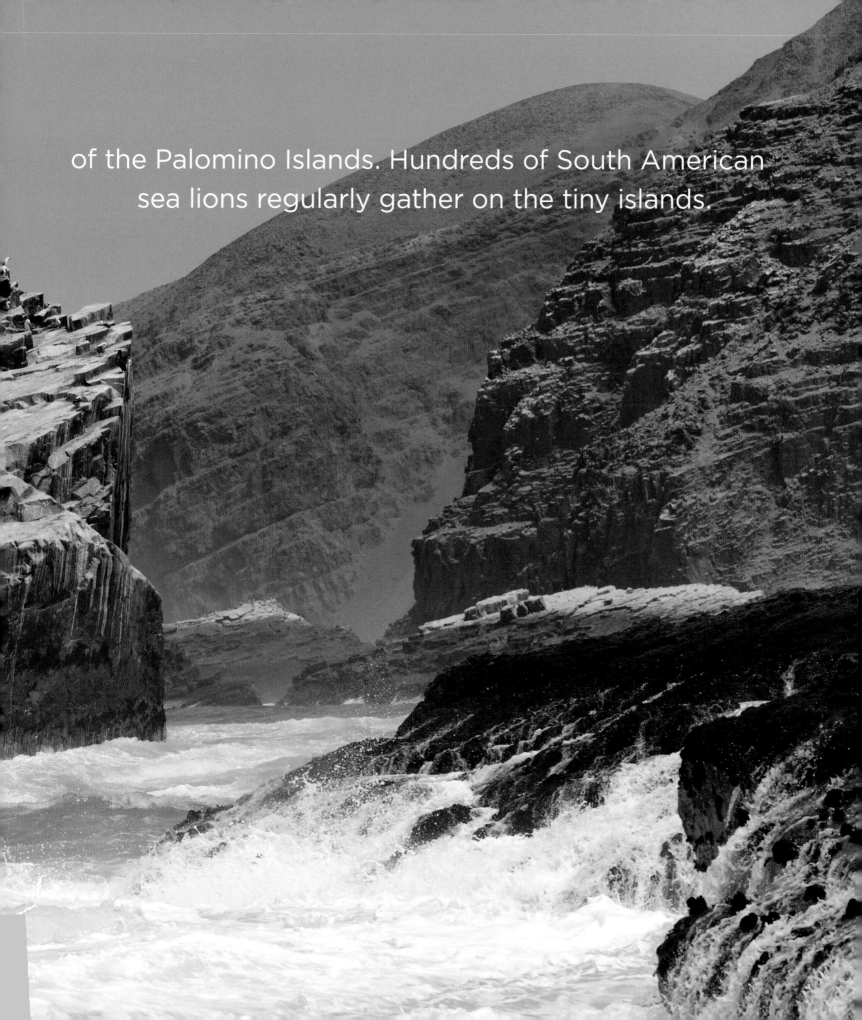

of the Palomino Islands. Hundreds of South American
sea lions regularly gather on the tiny islands.

On a January day in Lima, Peru, the early morning fog melts away under the sun, revealing the jagged shores of the Palomino Islands. Hundreds of South American sea lions regularly gather on the tiny islands. The animals budge each other with their massive chests, barking and grunting. Some dive into the water and then ride the ocean waves back to shore, playfully hauling themselves onto the rocks. Others recline on flat

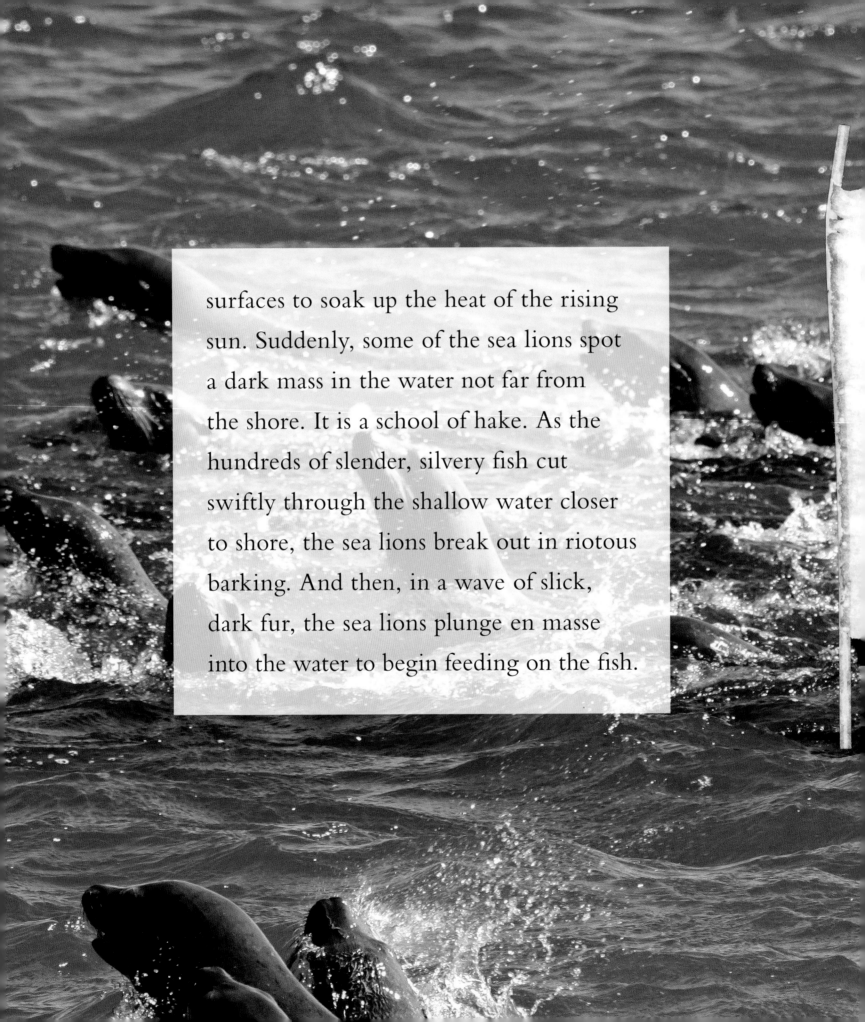

surfaces to soak up the heat of the rising
sun. Suddenly, some of the sea lions spot
a dark mass in the water not far from
the shore. It is a school of hake. As the
hundreds of slender, silvery fish cut
swiftly through the shallow water closer
to shore, the sea lions break out in riotous
barking. And then, in a wave of slick,
dark fur, the sea lions plunge en masse
into the water to begin feeding on the fish.

WHERE IN THE WORLD THEY LIVE

☐ **Australian Sea Lion**
Australia

☐ **California Sea Lion**
California, Oregon

■ **Galápagos Sea Lion**
Galápagos Islands

☐ **New Zealand Sea Lion**
New Zealand

■ **South American Sea Lion**
South America

■ **Steller Sea Lion**
North Pacific, Alaska

The six species of sea lion live along the coasts of three continents and several islands. In the Americas, California and Steller sea lions are found along the western North American coastline, while South American sea lions can be spotted from northern Peru to southern Brazil. Between the continents is a population of Galápagos sea lions, which breed on the Galápagos Islands. Australian sea lions live along the southwestern coast of that continent, and New Zealand sea lions are nearby on the island for which they're named.

OCEAN ACROBATS

Earless seals, sea lion relatives, lack ear flaps and hear through small holes on each side of the head.

The 33 living members of the Pinnipedia order, which includes sea lions, live mostly in cold-water coastal or island habitats around the world. Pinnipeds are characterized by their sleek bodies and wide, **webbed** flippers. The word "pinniped" is derived from the Latin *pinna*, meaning "wing" or "fin," and *pedis*, meaning "foot." This superfamily of fin-footed animals includes walruses and true, or earless, seals, as well as two groups of marine mammals that have ear flaps—eared seals. The nine fur seal species and six sea lion species are eared seals.

The six living sea lion species are the Australian, California, Galápagos, New Zealand, South American, and Steller. The Japanese sea lion was hunted to **extinction** in the 1950s. Sea lions earned their name hundreds of years ago from sailors who thought the fur around the necks of male South American sea lions looked like the manes of African lions. With the exception of the Steller sea lion, which was named after German naturalist Georg Wilhelm Steller, each species was named for its primary geographic location.

Their thick skin and dense fur protect sea lions from the jagged rocks on which they sun themselves.

Similar to dogs, which have hard nails at the end of each toe, sea lions have nails on the "toes" of their flippers.

Sea lions and their relatives are marine mammals, meaning they live mostly in the water and belong to a class of animals that, with the exceptions of the egg-laying platypus and hedgehog-like echidnas, give birth to live young and produce milk to feed them. Like all mammals, sea lions are warm-blooded. This means that their bodies maintain a constant temperature that is usually warmer than their surroundings. To help insulate its organs and protect itself against heat loss, the sea lion has a layer of thick fat, called blubber, just beneath its skin. Also, the sea lion's thick and coarse fur, called pelage (*PEH-lidge*), insulates the animal from the cold of its environment.

Like all mammals, sea lions rely on faster blood flow to increase their body temperature. Because the blood vessels in a sea lion's flippers are close to the skin's surface, a sea lion can speed up its blood flow while floating in the water by sticking a flipper up to capture the heat of the sun, thus helping warm its body. Dipping the flipper into the water and then raising it in the air helps cool the sea lion as the water **evaporates**, which is similar to the way humans sweat to cool off.

A sea lion may look as though it's waving, but it is more likely regulating its body temperature instead.

When on the lookout for food, sea lions may swim for up to 30 hours at a stretch without stopping to rest.

Sea lions and their relatives have long, streamlined bodies, a shape that allows for little **resistance** as the animals cut through the water, enabling them to dive, maneuver, and surface easily. Because of their similar general appearance, sea lions are sometimes confused with true seals. The main differences between the two animals can be found by observing the head and flippers. A true seal has only tiny openings for its ears, but a sea lion has small ear flaps. The ear flaps are pointed downward so water does not rush into the ears while the sea lion is swimming.

Secondly, true seals have short flippers. They use their rear flippers to propel their bodies through the water and their front flippers to steer. Sea lions have long flippers. Their front flippers are for swimming, while their rear flippers are for steering. The two animals move differently on land, too. True seals drag themselves or wriggle their bodies forward, but sea lions bend their back flippers forward and their front flippers backward to create a set of four feet on which to walk.

Male sea lions are called bulls, and females are called cows. The largest sea lion species is the Steller, which

Thanks to conservation efforts, the population of New Zealand fur seals is about 60,000 strong.

While fur seals grow longer than California sea lions by as much as 3 feet (0.9 m), they often weigh at least 100 pounds (45 kg) less.

Male Steller sea lions are highly vocal and typically bob their heads up and down when grumbling or roaring.

Adult sea lions molt annually, shedding and replacing their fur, and pups molt twice in their first six months of life.

is also called the northern sea lion. Mature Steller bulls can be 11 feet (3.4 m) long and 2,000 pounds (907 kg), though some may reach weights of up to 2,500 pounds (1,134 kg). Cows are much smaller, maxing out at almost 9 feet (2.7 m) and 1,000 pounds (454 kg). The Australian sea lion is the smallest species. Males of this species are no larger than Steller sea lion cows.

All sea lions are carnivores, meaning they eat meat from other animals such as fish, squid, crustaceans, penguins and other sea birds, and even small seals. An adult sea lion typically eats five to eight percent of its body weight in food each day, and it hunts and feeds exclusively in the water. Sea lions are the ocean's acrobats. Able to turn and spin sharply, sea lions maneuver swiftly and gracefully underwater. They charge into schools of fish, dive into rafts of swimming penguins, and spiral downward to the ocean floor to snatch crabs.

A mature sea lion has 34 to 38 teeth. It uses its sharp front teeth, called incisors, to snatch prey. Although the back teeth, called molars, are sharply ridged for crushing the shells of clams, crabs, and other crustaceans, sea lions do not chew their food, preferring instead to swallow

South American sea lions range in weight from about 330 pounds (150 kg) up to about 660 pounds (300 kg).

The sea lion's teeth, which are short but very sharp, can firmly hold wriggling, slippery prey such as fish.

their meals whole. A feeding sea lion will toss its prey upward and catch it in its mouth, letting the food slide down its throat. To keep from inhaling water when they dive, sea lions have special muscles in their noses that keep their nostrils in a naturally shut position until the sea lions consciously open them to breathe air.

Sea lions can dive as deep as 900 feet (274 m). Sea lion muscle has a high concentration of a substance called myoglobin, which enables oxygen to be stored and helps a sea lion stay underwater for long periods of time—up to 40 minutes. Underwater, sea lions hear as well as they do on land. Their eyesight is also strong, though scientists believe they may not see all colors of the **spectrum**. Like many **vertebrates**, such as cats, the sea lion has a layer of tissue called a tapetum lucidum behind each retina, the light-sensitive part of the inner eye. The tissue, which improves the animal's underwater vision, results in light being reflected off the eyes, an effect called eyeshine. In addition, a see-through inner eyelid called a nictitating (*NIK-tih-tayt-ing*) membrane closes over the sea lion's eyes to protect them from debris and sand.

Sea lions have sharp underwater vision but can see only bold outlines and general movements on land.

The stiff whiskers on a sea lion's face connect to sensitive nerves that can detect vibrations in the water while the sea lion hunts.

Even while hunting cooperatively, sea lions may be momentarily distracted by one of their favorite foods: sea urchins.

LIFE AT SEA

Sea lions are social animals and communicate with such sounds as clicks, chirps, groans, barks, and squeaks. They vocalize to establish territories, call out to family members, warn of predators, and signal food sources. Sea lions spend most of their time at sea, even sleeping while floating on their backs or bobbing with their back flippers pointed downward. When grouped together at sea, sea lions form what is called a raft. Sea lion rafts contain 15 to 20 members that hunt together.

Sea lions are cooperative hunters. They swim in circles around schools of fish, spiraling steadily tighter to force the fish into a compact mass. Then the sea lions plunge through the mass to snatch mouthfuls of fish. Sea lions have been observed working in this manner with seals and dolphins as well, sharing the bountiful feast.

On land, hundreds of sea lions may gather to sunbathe on rocky beaches or islands. Such groups are called colonies. A sea lion colony breaks apart during mating season, when the strongest bulls become dominant leaders. These bulls gather up as many cows as they can control to form new groups called harems. A harem may contain

Sea lion bulls may give barks of warning or fight each other viciously to defend their colonies or harems.

Sea lion pups often gather together to engage in playful fights that help them learn how to defend themselves when they get older.

The sea lion's sagittal crest is exterior evidence of how strong its jaw muscles are.

During mating season, male sea lions do not eat, living off their blubber instead and spending their time fending off rivals.

up to 15 cows and their offspring. Each bull defends the area where his harem rests and sunbathes, fending off the advances of rival bulls for an entire mating season, a period that lasts three months or longer. Bulls will bite each other, sometimes causing serious wounds, until one bull backs off.

Although maturity rate varies according to species, most sea lion cows begin mating at four to six years old, and bulls become old enough to mate when they reach eight to nine years old. Bulls this young rarely get to mate, though, because older, more powerful bulls chase them away from cows. Mature bulls have especially powerful jaws, a feature that is evidenced in the ridge of bone that protrudes across the top of their skulls. This bone is called a sagittal crest. Similar to the sagittal crest of mature male gorillas, this bone serves as the connecting point for one of the main chewing muscles. Sea lion bulls' sagittal crests reach full size at about 10 years of age.

The timing of mating season varies according to the species. California and Steller sea lions establish harems from May to July, and South American and New Zealand sea lions do so from November to January; however, Australian and Galápagos sea lions do not have as particular

Females cannot defend their pups against aggressive males, who may steal pups to show their dominance.

A bull typically maintains his territory and harem for two or three mating seasons before losing to a rival bull.

of a mating season and may breed anytime from May until January. Once a bull establishes a harem, it is up to his mature cows to initiate breeding. A cow will clamber over the bull's body, bite him in the neck, and then dash away as if trying to flee the harem. This sparks a possessive response in the bull, who then chases the female back to the harem, where he mates with her. Following this pattern, a dominant bull will mate with all the cows in his harem.

In all sea lion species, reproduction is tied to food supply. During times when food is scarce, a cow that becomes pregnant may put her baby, called a pup, "on hold" for three to five months. During this period, called embryonic diapause, the **embryo** stops developing until conditions improve or until the cow is able to travel to a better feeding area. This suspension of development ensures that the mother sea lion will have a food source while her pup is growing inside her. A sea lion cow that does not eat enough during her pregnancy may give birth prematurely to a dead pup.

The normal **gestation** period for sea lions is 11 to 12 months. Cows that are ready to give birth gather in the hundreds on rocky or sandy beaches. During this time, such areas are called rookeries. In the wild, sea lions give birth to a single pup. Evidence of twins has been observed only in zoos. Newborn pups are about 30 inches (76 cm) long and weigh about 13 pounds (6 kg). A pup cannot properly swim for the first two weeks of its life and cannot move quickly on land, which puts it at risk of being accidentally crushed by other sea lions. A pup relies on its mother for protection from jealous male sea lions that try to kill offspring that are not their own.

When a pup is first born, its mother barks at it repeatedly. The pup responds with bleats. In this way, the mother and her offspring learn each other's voices. The mother stays on land with her pup for four or five days. Then, she must go to sea in search of food. When she returns, she barks for her

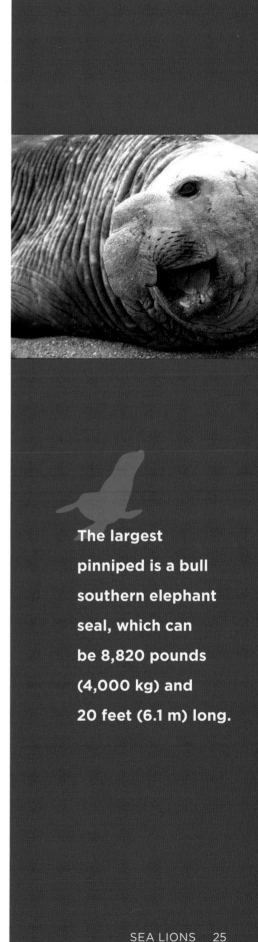

The largest pinniped is a bull southern elephant seal, which can be 8,820 pounds (4,000 kg) and 20 feet (6.1 m) long.

pup, who responds so that its mother can locate it among the hundreds of sea lion pups in the rookery. To make sure she has located the correct pup, a mother sea lion also relies on scent to identify her offspring.

Newborn pups have dark brown or black fur, which is shed and replaced with lighter brown fur over the first six months of the sea lion's life. Also, a pup is born with small baby teeth that fall out and are replaced with stronger permanent teeth when the sea lion is four months old. Because sea lions are mammals, they nurse their young with milk, which comes from four glands located behind the mother's front flippers. Depending on the species,

sea lion pups learn to catch fish at around two months of age, and while milk eventually becomes a minor part of a young sea lion's diet, it may take up to one year for a pup to stop nursing from its mother.

Female sea lions fiercely defend their young on land, but they cannot protect them from danger in the sea. The greatest threats to young sea lions are posed by sharks and killer whales—as well as a sea lion relative, the elephant seal, which can reach 20 feet (6.1 m) in length and easily swallow a young sea lion whole. In the wild, sea lions typically survive for up to 15 years, but in captivity, they can live twice that long.

Pups must remain close to their mothers near the edges of the colony to avoid being trampled by male sea lions.

A sea lion that displays aggression toward humans either wants to play or is defending its territory.

FULL OF FUN

Sea lions have played important roles in coastal cultures' traditions for thousands of years. The people of Peru once worshiped the sea lion as a symbol of life and of the sea's bounty. Today, they still embrace the sea lion as an important image in their artwork. Sea lion sculptures can be found as monuments to these creatures on the seashores of many other cities as well, including Sausalito and San Francisco in California, Mar del Plata in Argentina, and Florence in Oregon. Florence also features Sea Lion Caves, the world's largest sea cave, home to thousands of California and Steller sea lions.

Sea lions today are most recognizable not through art or in nature but in entertainment capacities. Performing sea lions are part of marine mammal exhibits at such places as Sea World and various zoos around the United States. Oceans of Fun is a marine mammal park in Milwaukee, Wisconsin, that specializes in sea lions, while Sea Lion Splash, based in Florida, is the only mobile sea lion exhibit in America. Sea Lion Splash travels the country with its eight California and South American sea lions, offering rare opportunities for people to interact with the acrobatic creatures.

The South American sea lion is the official symbol of Mar del Plata, Argentina, a major fishing port.

Sea lions played the character of a seal in Andre, *alongside actress Tina Majorino as Toni Whitney.*

When sea lions appear to be crying, the fluid dripping from their tear ducts is actually salt water being washed out of their bodies.

One of the performing sea lion's best-known tricks is balancing a ball on its nose. The truth is, however, that sea lions use their whiskers and not their noses to execute this feat. Even after she went blind, Breezy, the world's oldest captive sea lion, still enjoyed life in a "senior" pool at New York's Central Park Zoo. In 2006, though, both 36-year-old Breezy and her 31-year-old companion, Seaweed, passed away. Performing sea lions typically benefit from predator-free lives in captivity for many years.

Six captive California sea lions—Torey, Kalika, PJ, and three others—nearly lost their lives when Hurricane Katrina struck the Marine Life Oceanarium in Gulfport, Mississippi, in 2005. But like many captive animals that survived the disaster, the sea lions were relocated. They currently reside at Dolphin Encounters on Blue Lagoon, a wildlife park in the Bahamas. Before their move, in 1994, Torey, Kalika, and PJ appeared in the movie *Andre*, taking turns playing the title role in the true story of how a seal named Andre befriended a family in Rockport, Maine. The real Andre was a Maine harbor seal, but seals are difficult to train, so Torey, Kalika, and PJ played the part of Andre at different ages.

Sea lions are considered by many people to be the clowns of the sea. But this was not always the case. People once saw sea lions as little more than goods to be sold or traded. The practice of hunting sea lions and seals dates back thousands of years. Sea lions and other pinnipeds were at first a necessary food source for many coastal peoples, but as the centuries passed and civilizations grew, pinnipeds became valuable commodities. **Commercial** hunting in the 18th and 19th centuries provided fur and oil to people in developing cities. Like the waxy oil extracted from whale blubber, oil made from the fat of pinnipeds was used as fuel for lamps and material for making candles.

Performing sea lions are trained to exhibit various behaviors by being rewarded with fish.

Seals use their abdominal muscles to haul out, but sea lions use their front flippers to pull themselves upward.

The term "hauling out" is used to describe the action of a sea lion crawling out of the sea and onto land.

Although the demand for whale and pinniped oil declined with the widespread use of electric lights in the early 1900s, hunting for meat and fur continued into the mid-20th century. The North Pacific Fur Seal Treaty of 1911, which was signed by the U.S., Great Britain, Japan, and Russia, banned open-sea hunting and gave the U.S. power to regulate on-shore hunting of pinnipeds around the world. While international laws have changed over the past century, the U.S. remains a world leader in pinniped management and conservation. Still in place today are the U.S. Fur Seal Act of 1966—which stipulates that only members of certain **indigenous** tribes inhabiting the coastal areas of the North Pacific Ocean are allowed to **subsistence** hunt fur seals and sea otters—and the Marine Mammal Protection Act of 1972.

The sea lion's reputation as an intelligent ocean acrobat was sparked in 1919, when the British government revealed that it had been training California sea lions to hunt German submarines in the Atlantic Ocean. Britain's Royal Navy began training the sea lions in 1916 as part of its plan to combat German naval forces in World War I (1914–18). Sea lions were recognized as being highly

Sea lions earned the nickname "angels of the sea" for their graceful method of swimming.

California sea lions undergo harbor patrol training to detect swimmers near piers and ships for the SWIDS program.

intelligent and easily motivated by food. To train the sea lions, which had to be about three years old, a series of **conditioning** exercises was conducted, at first in a large pool and then in the open sea.

First, using food rewards, trainers taught the sea lions to locate the source of a buzzing sound. Next, the buzzing sound was combined with the sound of submarine propellers. The following step required the sea lions to drag buoys to mark the position of the sounds they located. The sea lions were taken to the open ocean for the final test: locating and marking a British submarine. The training had been a complete success—but not before the war ended in

1918. Seeing no further practical need for the sub-hunting sea lions, the British navy abandoned the project.

Later, in the 1950s, the U.S. Navy also began training sea lions and other marine mammals. Today, California sea lions are trained in San Diego to locate and mark underwater objects—including remote-controlled underwater devices and **mines**—and also to connect retrieval devices to these objects so that humans can pull them to the surface. Using techniques of positive reinforcement training similar to those used by the British navy decades earlier, the U.S. Navy's Marine Mammal Program uses sea lions to hunt not only objects but also people.

Just as guard dogs are used on land to protect restricted areas, so are sea lions used to patrol ships, piers, and harbors, warning against unauthorized human divers. Trained sea lions can even attach leg cuffs to a diver, immobilizing him so that military personnel can capture him with ease. As part of the highly successful Shallow Water Intruder Detection System (SWIDS), sea lions have been deployed to military bases on both U.S. coasts and in more than a dozen countries around the world.

The U.S. Navy keeps about 20 sea lions in active service to deliver tools and recover equipment for navy divers and civilian scientists.

Killer whales will ride a wave onto shore to grab sea lions and then ride the wave back to sea with their meal.

STRUGGLE TO SURVIVE

One of the earliest sea lion ancestors is now thought to be a semiaquatic otter-like creature that lived on land 24 to 20 million years ago. *Puijila darwini* was about three feet (0.9 m) long and had furry, webbed feet with claws. Species of another pinniped ancestor, *Enaliarctos*, lived even before *Puijila darwini* and gradually became better suited to life in the water. Its legs became flippers, and its tail disappeared. Its ears developed to hear underwater, and its whiskers became more sensitive, improving its underwater hunting abilities. *Enaliarctos* is believed to be the ancestor of all modern pinnipeds.

Today, sea lions' lives are filled with danger. They are preyed upon by sharks, killer whales, and elephant seals. They are illegally hunted for their meat, and they suffer from habitat disturbance and destruction. Recently, scientists have uncovered a great deal of information about the health issues that plague sea lions as well. Nursing pups are protected from disease by their mothers' immune systems, but adults may develop cancer, epilepsy, and pneumonia. Both captive and wild sea lions are affected in such ways, and once such

Puijila darwini *is considered an evolutionary link between land-dwelling mammals and aquatic seals and sea lions.*

Adult sea lions typically sleep about 12 hours a day, but pups need even more rest while they grow.

a health problem occurs, the afflicted sea lion rarely recovers—even with help from humans.

Research on California sea lions begun by the Marine Mammal Center in Sausalito in 1979 continues today. It has revealed that sea lions develop the same forms of cancer as those found in human smokers or people exposed to heavy amounts of cancer-causing toxins. In addition, current studies on dead sea lions have revealed the presence of pollutants such as **DDT** and **PCBs** in their blubber, and further research indicates such toxins can affect the development of pups' **hormones** and internal organs before they are even born.

Parasites pose another health risk to sea lions. Little can be done to prevent or treat parasites in wild sea lions. The number of sea lions troubled with parasites, which are hardier in warmer waters, has increased in recent years. Scientists believe this has to do with global warming. As ocean temperatures have risen above normal levels, parasite populations have increased. Sea lions living in warm-water habitats have thus become more susceptible to parasites.

Declines in sea lion populations can also be attributed to global warming-related starvation in some cases. Some scientists believe that the normal cycle of rising and falling ocean temperatures, caused by the weather pattern known as El Niño (which typically occurs every three to seven years), has been altered by the effects of global warming. Extended El Niño conditions affect ocean habitats around the world. As ocean temperatures rise sharply, the fish and squid on which many sea lions feed seek out cooler places in deeper waters—where sea lions cannot reach them—resulting in the starvation of entire colonies of sea lions.

Pups, which find hunting for food under normal circumstances challenging, are especially vulnerable to

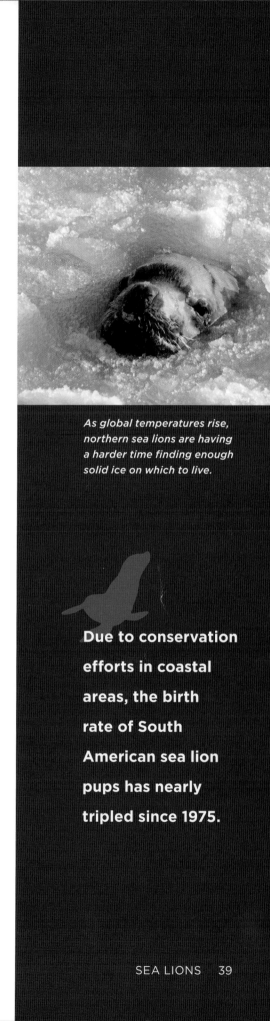

As global temperatures rise, northern sea lions are having a harder time finding enough solid ice on which to live.

Due to conservation efforts in coastal areas, the birth rate of South American sea lion pups has nearly tripled since 1975.

When pups go without food, their bodies take nutrition from their blubber and muscle, leaving the pups thin and sickly.

changes in their habitat. In 2009, hundreds of dead or dying California sea lion pups began washing up on beaches along the West Coast from Oregon to Southern California. Despite the efforts of workers from rescue centers such as Pacific Marine Mammal Center in Laguna Beach, California, who captured and treated many of the stranded pups, most of the animals were too sick to survive.

Similar problems have been affecting other sea lion species, the pups of which have been washing up on South American beaches from Patagonia to Argentina and on the subarctic shores of the Auckland Islands near New Zealand. While the normal **mortality rate** of sea lion pups is around 30 percent, researchers believe that it has spiked to 80 percent in recent years for certain populations.

In order to help sea lions survive in a changing climate, a number of institutions are looking to healthy sea lions for clues as to why some sea lions are thriving while others are dying. The Steller sea lion, which lives in the cold waters off Alaska's coast, shows no signs of starvation; however, this sea lion species is also in serious decline. Conservationists blame Alaska's fishing industry for depleting the Steller sea lion's food sources, but researchers

have found little proof that this is true. Fishermen blame killer whales for reducing the Steller sea lion population, but no evidence of this has been presented, either.

Since 2003, a program operated by Dr. Jo-Ann Mellish of the Alaska SeaLife Center (ASLC) has monitored sea lion health. To do this, the program has captured hundreds of young Steller sea lions to study. In a relatively painless procedure, each sea lion is put to sleep using anesthesia, and a small electronic transmitter is then surgically implanted in the blubber covering its stomach, just under the skin. The transmitter, which runs on a battery that lasts up to two years, sends out data through a signal that is picked up by a satellite. The device records heart rate, body temperature, and other physical processes.

The paint used to tag seals and sea lions for population tracking typically lasts about three months before wearing off.

Steller sea lions are mighty hunters, often preying on harbor seals, ringed seals, and fur seals as well as on sea otter pups.

The goal of ASLC's research is to determine the reasons for the decline of the Steller sea lion population before it is too late to save these creatures.

Other research projects are looking for answers to a different question. The Alaska Department of Fish and Game (ADF&G) has been trying to figure out why the population of Steller sea lions is so high on South Marble Island in Glacier Bay. A radio antenna attached with temporary glue to the top of a sea lion's head provides the ADF&G with about 80 days' worth of data on the sea lion's movements. Tagging and monitoring dozens of sea lions in this way may offer clues about the survival tactics used by the colony of sea lions on Marble Island, helping researchers develop conservation strategies for sea lion colonies elsewhere.

Wherever sea lions are found, they must compete with humans for the ocean's resources. Garbage dumping, toxic chemicals, industrial oil spills, and overfishing represent just some of the challenges that sea lions face. Continued research and education on the needs and habits of sea lions can help these marine mammals survive on this ever-changing planet.

Each sea lion smells different, so sea lions sniff the air to recognize each other and locate their pups.

ANIMAL TALE: THE SEA LION WIFE

The Ainu people settled the Japanese island of Hokkaidō 20,000 years ago. They believe that every living thing is endowed with *kamuy*, or spirit. This ancient Ainu tale explains the special relationship between fishers and sea lions.

One day long ago, a man went fishing for salmon. On the seashore, he saw a heap of beautiful fur coats piled on a rock. Seeing no one around, and thinking the furs were too lovely to resist, the man snatched one of the coats. He hurried home with it and locked it in a chest.

When the man returned to the river, all the fur coats were gone, and in their place sat a young woman. She was shivering, for she had no clothes. The man, feeling sorry for the woman, took her home, bundled her in a blanket, and fed her hot soup, after which the woman fell asleep. The man thought she was the most beautiful woman he'd ever seen and decided that he would ask her to marry him.

The next day, he did just that, and the woman agreed. They lived happily together for many years, and the woman gave birth to many beautiful children. After 20 years, the man wanted to celebrate his marriage by giving his wife a gift. He remembered the fur coat he had found 20 years earlier.

Pulling the coat from the chest, the man declared, "This is a gift for you, my lovely wife." He pressed the luxurious fur into his wife's hands. The woman cried out in surprise and joy, for the coat was already hers. She and her siblings, the sea lions, had swum to shore and taken off their coats to walk in the forest as humans for a time. When they had returned to the shore, her coat was missing, and so she could not return to the sea.

"You have given me 20 years of joy on land," said the woman, "but now that I have my coat, I must return to the sea."

The man was suddenly saddened. He did not mean to deprive his wife of her coat as a young woman, but he also did not wish to lose her now. "You must leave me?" he asked.

"I must," his wife replied as she tenderly kissed him. Then she slipped into her fur coat and was instantly transformed into a sea lion.

The heartbroken man followed his wife to the seashore. He did not know what he regretted more: taking the coat 20 years ago or giving it back to his wife that day. The sea lion plunged into the icy water and swam in joyous circles. She was home. Raising a flipper out of the water, she waved at her husband. And then she dipped below the waves and was gone.

For the rest of his life, whenever the man went fishing for salmon, his wife the sea lion would greet him. The man would throw the heads of the salmon he caught out to her as gifts. While there are no more sea lions in Japan, other sea lions around the world still eagerly accept the gifts of fish heads that fishers toss out to them.

GLOSSARY

commercial – used for business and to gain a profit rather than for personal reasons

conditioning – a process of training living things to behave in a certain way

DDT – a chemical compound used to kill pest insects that was later found to cause health problems in people who lived in the environments where it was used

embryo – an unborn or unhatched offspring in its early stages of development

evaporates – changes from liquid to invisible vapor, or gas

extinction – the act or process of becoming extinct; coming to an end or dying out

gestation – the period of time it takes a baby to develop inside its mother's womb

hormones – chemical substances produced in the body that control and regulate the activity of certain cells and organs

indigenous – originating in a particular region or country

mines – explosive devices left in a place that are triggered by the approach of

or contact with objects such as submarines or tanks

mortality rate – the number of deaths in a certain area or period

parasites – animals or plants that live on or inside another living thing (called a host) while giving nothing back to the host; some parasites cause disease or even death

PCBs – chemical compounds that once were used abundantly in manufacturing and are now illegal because of their toxic and long-lasting effects on living things and their offspring

resistance – the slowing effect applied by one thing against another

spectrum – a range of qualities in related items such as light waves or sound waves

subsistence – relating to production of something at a small-scale level, without extra to trade

vertebrates – animals that have a backbone, including mammals, birds, reptiles, amphibians, and fish

webbed – connected by a web (of skin, as in the case of webbed feet)

SELECTED BIBLIOGRAPHY

Braje, Todd J., and Torben C. Rick, eds. *Human Impacts on Seals, Sea Lions, and Sea Otters: Integrating Archaeology and Ecology in the Northeast Pacific.* Berkeley: University of California Press, 2011.

Marine Mammal Center. "The Pinnipeds: Seals, Sea Lions, and Walruses." http://www .marinemammalcenter.org/education/marine-mammal-information/pinnipeds.

Quirks, Joe. *Call to the Rescue: The Story of the Marine Mammal Center.* San Francisco: Chronicle Books, 2009.

San Diego Zoo. "Animal Bytes: Sea Lion." http://www .sandiegozoo.org/animalbytes/t-sea_lion.html.

Stewart, Brent S., James A. Powell, Phillip J. Clapham, and Randall R. Reeves. *Sea Mammals of the World: A Complete Guide to Whales, Dolphins, Seals, Sea Lions and Sea Cows.* London: Christopher Helm Publishers, 2002.

Trites, A. W. *Sea Lions of the World.* Fairbanks: Alaska Sea Grant College Program, 2006.

Sea lions bark to communicate with each other, and they teach their young this communication as well.

INDEX